W9-CAP-603

Contents

n princ

G005 188

The Apostles' Creed

Text by Inos Biffi
Illustrations by Franco Vignazia

WILLIAM B. EERDMANS PUBLISHING COMPANY
GRAND RAPIDS, MICHIGAN

Originally published as
Il Credo, copyright © 1992
Editoriale Jaca Book spa, Milan.

English translation copyright © 1994
by Wm. B. Eerdmans Publishing Co.
255 Jefferson Ave. S.E., Grand Rapids, Mich. 49503

All rights reserved

Printed in Italy

Library of Congress Cataloging-in-Publication Data

Biffi, Inos.
[Credo. English]
The Apostles' Creed / text by Inos Biffi ; illustrations by Franco Vignazia.
p. cm.
ISBN 0-8028-3756-5
1. Apostles' Creed—Juvenile literature.
2. Catholic Church—Doctrines—Juvenile literature.
[1. Apostles' Creed. 2. Catholic Church—Doctrines.]
I. Vignazia, Franco, ill. II. Title.
BT993.2.B5413 1993
238′.11—dc20   93-39151
                                                     CIP
                                                     AC

Imprimatur
in Curia Arch. Mediolani die 9 Junii 1992
Angelus Mascheroni
provicarius generalis

INOS BIFFI is Professor of Medieval and Systematic Theology at the
Theological University of Northern Italy, Milan.

FRANCO VIGNAZIA lives in Italy and is an illustrator, painter, and
sculptor. He also teaches art in the secondary schools.

Unless otherwise indicated, all Scripture quotations are from the New American Bible,
© 1986 Confraternity of Christian Doctrine, Washington, D.C.

Introduction

The purpose of this book is very simple: to teach Christian children the Apostles' Creed. For everyone, regardless of age, the Apostles' Creed is the symbol of faith, its identification card, so to speak. As we become adults and gradually develop a deeper understanding of faith, we are simply expanding our understanding of the precepts of the Apostles' Creed, in its precise and precious formulas, which are ancient yet always new, and which were developed almost immediately and with great care by the Church. The Church repeats them always and never ceases to find new meaning in them.

For children, memorizing the Apostles' Creed represents a significant and beneficial contact with the faith of their parents, of the Christian community in which they live. This book is designed so that parents or other adults can guide children through the explanation of the Apostles' Creed offered here, expanding upon the content with their own comments. They will transmit with confidence and passion the faith that they in turn have received, knowing that they now can draw happily and fully upon the Catechism of the Catholic Church.

The illustrations that accompany the text are direct and simple. This encourages children to visualize what they are reading and hearing. We hope that this synthesis of text and pictures will make the instruction here clear and concrete, and that faith will take root in both the minds and the hearts of the children who study this book, so that they may grow in both knowledge of the faith and good works.

Jesus Sends His Disciples to Proclaim the Gospel

When Jesus rose from the dead, before he ascended into heaven to be near his Father, he sent his disciples — those individuals who were his followers — to proclaim to all people the joyous announcement of salvation, which is the Gospel. After Jesus ascended into heaven, he sent the Holy Spirit to accompany the disciples on this mission. Those people who had faith would be saved.

The Teachers of Faith
—the Apostles

Jesus had many disciples, and from among them he chose the twelve apostles. Peter was the first apostle and the leader of the group. The apostles did not replace Jesus but were his representatives here on earth. (Of course, Jesus is always present in the Church.) In Jesus' name, and with the authority that they received from him, the apostles governed the church. The bishops are the successors of the apostles. They are led by the bishop of Rome, the Pope, who is the successor of Peter. Those who listen to them listen to Jesus Christ.

I believe in God,

the Father Almighty,

Forever and above all, there is God — one God in three Persons: the Father, the Son, and the Holy Spirit. Therefore, forever and above all, there is the Trinity. No one has ever seen God, except Jesus, the Son of God. By coming to earth and becoming a man, Jesus revealed God to us. When Jesus was baptized, God clearly indicated his relationship with him. The heavens opened, and the Holy Spirit descended upon Jesus in the form of a dove, and a voice spoke. It was the voice of the Father, who said, "This is my beloved son" (Matt. 3:17). This is the main precept of the Apostles' Creed.

Creator of heaven
and earth,

God is all-powerful. He is the Creator who freely made all things from nothing — visible, like plants and animals, and invisible, like the angels. There was nothing until he created it. And without him, nothing would exist.

God is Love, and he looks after his creatures with love — particularly us, because we are made in his image. God is not the source of evil. Evil came into the world because of the rebellious angels like Satan and because of the disobedience of the first man, Adam. Because of Adam, all of us are born with the sign of that sin: the original sin.

and in Jesus Christ, his only Son, our Lord,

God is the Father, and from eternity, Jesus Christ is his Son, the second Person of the Trinity. Saint John, the evangelist, said of Jesus, "In the beginning was the Word [meaning Jesus, who testified to God's existence], and the Word was with God, and the Word was God. He was in the beginning with God. All things came to be through him, and without him nothing came to be. What came to be through him was life, and this life was the light of the human race" (John 1:1-4). Jesus was the cause, the model, and the purpose of creation. And in a special way, man and woman were created in his image. Jesus is the Lord of all, because he loves and offers salvation to everyone, even those who do not yet know him.

who was
conceived by the
Holy Spirit,

born of the Virgin Mary,

Jesus is the Son of God who became a true man. He was born in Bethlehem to Mary and Joseph. Jesus was miraculously conceived by the Holy Spirit, because God can do all things. Mary, Jesus' mother, carried Jesus in her womb with faith and love, and Saint Joseph, her husband, looked after Jesus with the love of a father.

suffered under Pontius Pilate, was crucified, died . . .

Jesus spent his life preaching the Gospel, pardoning sinners, casting out demons, healing the sick, revealing the Father's love for everyone, and instructing people to love one another. This was what his Father wanted him to do, but there were people in power who didn't believe in him, so he was condemned to death. He was condemned above all because he proclaimed himself to be the Son of God. By making this declaration and standing by it, Jesus remained faithful to God, and by dying on the cross he offered himself to God as a sign of love, as a sacrifice for our sins. Because of this, our sins are forgiven, and we receive the grace to become children of God. Jesus himself had declared that he had not come into this world to be served, but rather to serve others and to give his life in order to free all people.

Because of Adam's disobedience, we were lost, but because of Jesus' obedience, we are saved.

. . . and was buried.
He descended into hell.

After Jesus died, his body was removed from the
cross and taken to a tomb, which remained sealed
for three days. But the soul of Jesus descended into
hell, into the realm of the dead. There he freed
those who had waited for him as their Redeemer,
and he took them to heaven, to be near his Father,

in the joy of eternal life. Jesus also proclaimed the Gospel to them and announced the grace of salvation, which had been accomplished by his death on the cross. In this way, the patriarchs — Abraham, Isaac, and Jacob — the prophets, and righteous people who had lived before Jesus' time were able to enter Paradise.

The third day he rose again from the dead.

Jesus conquered death and rose again after three days, leaving his tomb empty (Mark 16:6). In his glorified body, he appeared to selected followers. At first they doubted that the figure before them was their leader, but soon they became joyously convinced that the crucified Christ was indeed alive. The disciples walked with Jesus and talked with him and ate with him, and they bear witness to the fact that Jesus came back from the dead, and wasn't just a phantom or a beautiful dream.

It is extremely important that Jesus did not remain in the tomb. If he had not risen from the dead, our entire faith would be pointless and without foundation. But by conquering the grave, he conquered sin and saved us.

He ascended into heaven,

Before he returned to heaven, the risen Jesus remained close to his disciples for forty days. He helped them to understand the sacred Scriptures that had predicted his passion and resurrection from the grave. He explained to them God's plan for the conversion and salvation of humanity. And

by offering the disciples proof that he was truly alive, he reinforced their certainty about his resurrection, so that they could testify to his resurrection without the slightest shadow of doubt.

Finally, Jesus entrusted the disciples with this mission: "Go, therefore, and make disciples of all nations, baptizing them in the name of the Father, and of the Son, and of the Holy Spirit, teaching them to observe all that I have commanded you" (Matt. 28:19-20). And after he told them that he would be with them always, he ascended into heaven.

and sits at the right hand of God, the Father Almighty.

When Jesus ascended into heaven, he was welcomed with great rejoicing by his Father. He had sent Jesus to earth as a gift to us, to bring us salvation. Now, after enduring the humiliation of the cross and triumphing over the grave, Jesus entered the same glory as God the Father, who rewarded him and honored him for his obedience. In the glorified Jesus, all of humanity is exalted. He represents the goal and the heavenly destiny of all humanity, whom he calls to himself. His ascension did not mean that he had abandoned us or distanced himself from us. As he promised, "I am with you always, until the end of the age" (Matt. 28:20).

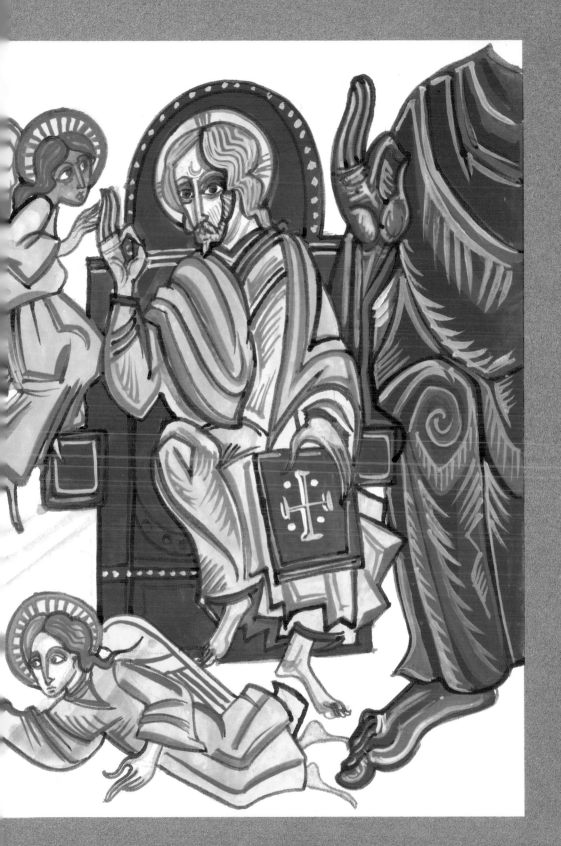

From thence
he shall
come to
judge
the
living
and
the
dead.

At the end of time, Jesus will come to judge all humankind. Only God knows the time of this second coming. But even though we do not see Jesus now as he will appear then, in his glorious manifestation, he is always present here on earth, and he can appear at any moment. And we know that we will see him on the day that we die. What is important right now is to live like his faithful and watchful disciples, keeping hope alive while we wait for him. All authority and power in heaven and on earth belong to him. He will closely judge the life and the actions of every human being. Through his judgment, which is both merciful and final, each person will receive eternal rewards in heaven or eternal suffering in hell.

I believe in
the Holy Spirit,

After he had ascended into heaven, the Lord Jesus, together with his Father, sent the Holy Spirit, the third Person of the Trinity, to his followers on the feast of Pentecost. The Holy Spirit was already at work in the world: he had participated in the creation, and had appeared in the form of a dove at Jesus' baptism, and was inspiring the writing of the Holy Scriptures. It is the Holy Spirit who now makes Jesus present in the world and teaches us to know and love him.

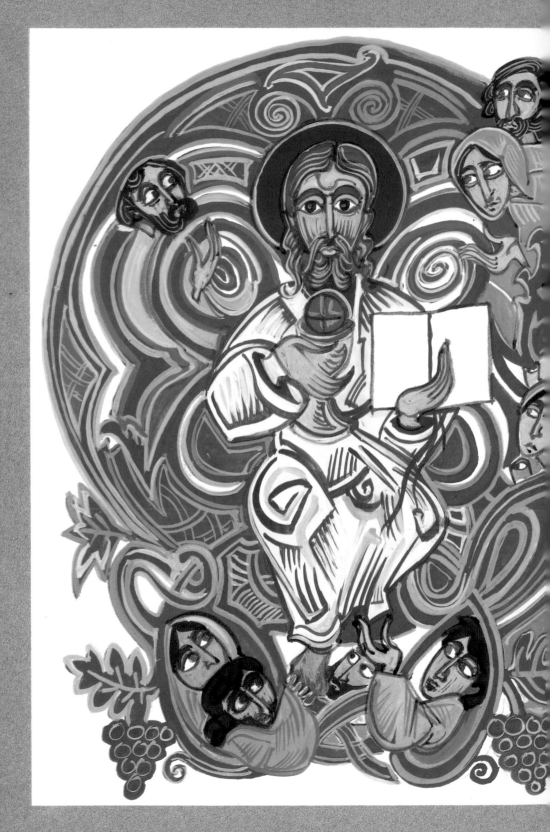

the holy Catholic Church,

The Church came into being on Pentecost, when the Father, through his glorified Son, Jesus, sent the Holy Spirit upon Jesus' followers. The Church is formed by those who convert, who believe in the Gospel, who are baptized, who are strengthened by the Lord through the Eucharist, and who live like children of God. All of this is possible through the grace of the Holy Spirit, who makes us recognize Jesus and inspires faith in him. It is the Holy Spirit who regenerates those who are baptized; it is the Holy Spirit who transforms bread and wine into the

Body and Blood of Christ during the Eucharist; it is the Holy Spirit who lives in the hearts of the faithful and makes their actions conform to those of Jesus.

The Church is the people of God; it is the body of Christ. The Church is one, even though there are many Christian communities around the world, because it is united by Jesus through the Holy Spirit. The Church is holy because it was formed by the followers of God, who were

sanctified by the Holy Spirit. The Church is catholic because all people are called to be part of it. The Church is apostolic because it was founded upon the testimonies of the apostles, who were succeeded by the bishops, led by the head bishop, the Pope.

The Church is the effective and necessary sign for salvation. Those who sincerely seek God already begin to belong to the Church in their hearts. All of the holiness and beauty of the Church will be perfected in heaven.

the communion of Saints,

The Church is a community of saints. Those who are already in heaven intercede on our behalf, together with Mary, the mother of Jesus and the mother of us all. Together with the saints in heaven, there are the faithful, the pilgrims on earth, who share the same faith, the same body of Christ, the same Spirit. Even the dead who are being purified in Purgatory are members of this one family of God.

the forgiveness

When we are born, we do not yet possess the dignity and sanctity of children of God. Instead, our souls all mysteriously bear the sign of the sin of Adam, which is sadly renewed in each sin that we commit. But the risen Jesus gave us the Holy Spirit for the forgiveness of sins, which he earned for us through his death on the cross. God offers everyone the grace of forgiveness. The Church is

# of sins,

the sign of that forgiveness and the effective instrument of that forgiveness in the world by means of the sacraments of baptism and confession. When the Church administers baptism to people, all their sins are forgiven and they are reborn through the water and the Holy Spirit as children of God. And through the sacrament of confession the Church forgives the sins of those who confess them with sincere repentance. The grace of forgiveness is offered to everyone and for all time.

the resurrection

Death came into the world as a punishment for sin. By rising again from the dead, Jesus overcame sin and death for all humankind. All those who live and die in communion with Jesus, who is "the resurrection and the life" (John 11:25), carry within them the seed of resurrection. Because of this, the Holy Spirit can raise them up in the image of the Lord, who was the first to have risen from the dead. Their bodies will also be saved — they will be whole people, united body and soul, in their glory. However, those who die in mortal sin shall be raised from the dead not to enjoy eternal life but to suffer damnation.

of the body,

and life everlasting. Amen.

When those who live their lives as children of God die and face the final judgment, they will enter into eternal life, and, together with Jesus and the saints, they will know the unimaginable joy of seeing the Father. But those who have obstinately refused the salvation that God offers to everyone will be condemned to eternal suffering. Purgatory is the place where believers can undergo a final purification before seeing God.

LTSS Lineberger Memorial Library

3 5898 00107 8688

PZ 7 .B54 Apo 1994
Biffi, Inos.
The Apostles' Creed

LINEBERGER
MEMORIAL LIBRARY
LUTHERAN THEOLOGICAL
SOUTHERN SEMINARY
COLUMBIA, SOUTH CAROLINA 29203

DEMCO